SIBERIAN TIGER VS. SABER-TOOTH CAT

BY CHARLES C. HOFER

CAPSTONE PRESS
a capstone imprint

Published by Capstone Press, an imprint of Capstone.
1710 Roe Crest Drive, North Mankato, Minnesota 56003
capstonepub.com

Library of Congress Cataloging-in-Publication Data
Names: Hofer, Charles, author.
Title: Siberian tiger vs. saber-tooth cat / by Charles C. Hofer.
Description: North Mankato, Minnesota : Capstone Press, [2024] | Series: Beastly battles | Includes bibliographical references and index. | Audience: Ages 9-11 Audience: Grades 4-6
Summary: "It's a battle between two fearsome, fanged beasts! Today, the Siberian tiger holds the record as the world's biggest cat. But in prehistoric times, the saber-tooth cat held that title as it prowled the land for prey. Learn what makes these similar animals such effective hunters. Then decide which fierce fighter would best the other in battle"— Provided by publisher.
Identifiers: LCCN 2023019035 (print) | LCCN 2023019036 (ebook) | ISBN 9781669065104 (hardcover) | ISBN 9781669065180 (paperback) | ISBN 9781669065142 (pdf) | ISBN 9781669065203 (kindle edition) | ISBN 9781669065197 (epub)
Subjects: LCSH: Siberian tiger—Juvenile literature. | Saber-toothed tigers—Juvenile literature.
Classification: LCC QL737.C23 H614 2024 (print) | LCC QL737.C23 (ebook) DDC 599.756—dc23/eng/20230717
LC record available at https://lccn.loc.gov/2023019035
LC ebook record available at https://lccn.loc.gov/2023019036

Editorial Credits
Editor: Aaron Sautter; Designer: Bobbie Nuytten; Media Researcher: Rebekah Hubstenberger: Production Specialist: Whitney Schaefer

Image Credits
Alamy: Benny Marty, 5 (bottom), Stocktrek Images, Inc., 17, 19, 27 (top), 23, 24, Universal Images Group North America LLC/DeAgostini, 11; Getty Images: Ibrahim Suha Derbent, 5 (top), iStock/Andyworks, Cover (top), 13, iStock/Freder, 20, iStock/Kantapatp, 28, iStock/ViktorCap, 8, Kathleen Reeder Wildlife Photography, 21, Mike Hill, 15; Shutterstock: Daniel Eskridge, Cover (bottom), GUDKOV ANDREY, 7, Kutikova Ekaterina, 9, Nicolas Primola, 6, Sergey Uryadnikov, 27 (bottom), Stanislav Duben, 25, Vac1, 29

Printed and bound in the USA. PO 5626

TABLE OF CONTENTS

READY . . . SET . . . FIGHT! 4

BEASTLY BRAWLERS 6

ONE BIG KITTY. .8

TERRIBLE TEETH 10

A GIANT BITE 12

KILLER CLAWS. .14

NO ESCAPE 16

SUPER-SIZED SABER-TOOTH 18

A POWERFUL PREDATOR 20

SNEAK ATTACK. .22

SLY HUNTERS 24

FELINE FIGHT! 26

WHO'S THE WINNER? 28

GLOSSARY. 30

READ MORE .31

INTERNET SITES 31

INDEX 32

ABOUT THE AUTHOR. 32

Words in **bold** are in the glossary.

READY . . . SET . . . FIGHT!

Are you ready for a battle between big cats? These ferocious **felines** are ready to fight.

Saber-tooth cats lived millions of years ago. They were the top cats of their time.

Siberian tigers are big and powerful too. Which fierce beast will win?

SIBERIAN TIGER

SABER-TOOTH CAT

BEASTLY BRAWLERS

The Siberian tiger and saber-tooth cat have a lot in common. They're both big, bad cats. They have sharp claws and big teeth. They're expert **predators**. They use their speed and strength to catch **prey**.

ONE BIG KITTY

Siberian tigers are huge. They're the world's largest cat. They're bigger than jaguars or panthers. They're even bigger than African lions.

Most pet house cats weigh about 10 pounds (4.5 kilograms). But a Siberian tiger can weigh up to 900 pounds (408 kg). That's one *big* kitty!

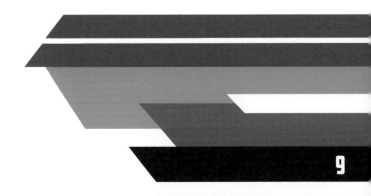

TERRIBLE TEETH

The saber-tooth cat is known for its huge teeth. Its **canine teeth** grew up to 8 inches (20 centimeters) long. They were curved like a sword called a saber. The cat's long teeth might have helped cut **flesh** from its prey.

A GIANT BITE

The Siberian tiger has large teeth too. Its canines can be up to 3 inches (7.2 cm) long.

These tigers are known for their powerful bite. Their jaws are so strong that they can snap bones.

The saber-tooth cat had a much smaller jaw. The cat's bite was dangerous. But it was weak compared to the Siberian tiger.

KILLER CLAWS

The Siberian tiger has sharp claws—and they're huge! They can be up to 4 inches (10.1 cm) long. Their claws help capture and hold prey.

Like all cats, the tiger's claws are **retractable**. This helps keep them sharp and deadly.

NO ESCAPE

The saber-tooth cat also had big, sharp claws. They were about the same size as the Siberian tiger's claws. The saber-tooth used its claws to catch prey like bison and camels.

The saber-tooth had strong front legs. They helped the cat hold onto its prey. There was no escaping a saber-tooth's powerful claws and legs.

SUPER-SIZED SABER-TOOTH

Saber-tooth cats were huge. It was one of the largest hunters of its time. The saber-tooth cat weighed up to 750 pounds (340 kg).

Saber-tooths had to be big. They competed for food with other big hunters. These included the dire wolf and short-faced bear.

A SABER-TOOTH CAT DEFENDS ITS PREY FROM DIRE WOLVES.

A POWERFUL PREDATOR

The Siberian tiger likes to **ambush** its prey. It hides in the forest. When the prey walks by—it pounces!

Tigers can run up to 60 miles (97 kilometers) per hour. This helps them to chase and catch their prey. Not many animals can escape the tiger's attack.

SNEAK ATTACK

Saber-tooth cats probably **stalked** their prey. They followed prey slowly. The big cats stayed quiet and hid. Then, at the right moment, they attacked! With their powerful claws and large teeth, other animals didn't stand a chance.

23

SLY HUNTERS

Saber-tooth cats were **social** animals. They may have hunted in packs, like wolves do today. They could have worked together to kill large prey. This **strategy** probably helped the big cats survive.

Siberian tigers are **solitary** cats. They hunt alone. They don't like being around other tigers.

FELINE FIGHT!

Five fierce fighters face-off deep in a forest. A Siberian tiger is surrounded by several hungry saber-tooth cats. The saber-tooths growl and hiss. They show off their long teeth.

But then the tiger responds. **ROAR!** This tells its enemies, "Back off!"

It's time for a big cat battle!

27

WHO'S THE WINNER?

You've met two big killer cats. The Siberian tiger is a powerful predator. The saber-tooth cat is an ancient master hunter. Which beast would win this clash of big cats?

	Siberian Tiger	**Saber-Tooth Cat**
HABITAT	mountain forests of Asia	forests and grasslands of North America
WEIGHT	900 pounds (408 kg)	up to 750 pounds (340 kg)
LENGTH	up to 12 feet (3.7 m)	about 5.5 feet (1.7 m)
SPEED	60 mph (97 kph)	unknown
WEAPONS	• teeth, 3 inches (7.6 cm) long • claws, 4 inches (10.1 cm) long • very strong bite	• teeth, 8 inches (20 cm) long • claws, 4 inches (10.1 cm) long • strong legs
DEFENSES	sharp claws, speedy runner	sharp claws, lived in groups
STRATEGY	stalks prey alone	hunted in packs

GLOSSARY

ambush (AM-bush)—a surprise attack

canine teeth (KAY-nine TEETH)—pointed teeth that help tear food into smaller pieces

feline (FEE-line)—any animal of the cat family

flesh (FLESH)—the soft parts of the body that cover the bones, such as skin and muscles

predator (PRED-uh-tur)—an animal that hunts other animals for food

prey (PRAY)—an animal that is hunted and eaten by another animal

retractable (rih-TRAK-tuh-buhl)—able to slide in and out

social (SOH-shuhl)—living in groups or packs

solitary (SOL-uh-ter-ee)—living and hunting alone

stalk (STAWK)—to hunt an animal in a quiet, secret way

strategy (STRAT-uh-jee)—a plan or method of achieving a goal

READ MORE

Clay, Kathryn. *Saber-toothed Cat.* North Mankato, MN: Capstone Press, 2018.

Gish, Ashley. *Saber-toothed Cats.* Mankato, MN: The Creative Company, 2023.

Hansen, Grace. *Siberian Tigers.* Minneapolis: Abdo Kids Jumbo, 2019.

INTERNET SITES

DK Find Out: Smilodon
dkfindout.com/us/dinosaurs-and-prehistoric-life/prehistoric-mammals/smilodon/

Fact Animal: Siberian Tiger Facts
factanimal.com/siberian-tiger/

Kiddle: Saber-toothed Cat Facts for Kids
kids.kiddle.co/Saber–toothed_cat

INDEX

dire wolves, 18

house cats, 9

saber-tooth cats
  bite, 12
  claws, 6, 16, 22, 29
  habitat, 29
  hunting strategies, 22, 24, 29
  legs, 16, 29
  prey, 6, 10, 16, 19, 22, 24
  range, 29
  size, 18, 29
  speed, 6, 29
  teeth, 6, 10, 22, 26, 29
  time on Earth, 4

short-faced bears, 18
Siberian tigers
  bite, 12, 29
  claws, 6, 14, 29
  habitat, 29
  hunting strategies, 20–21, 25, 29
  prey, 6, 14, 20, 21, 29
  range, 29
  size, 8–9, 29
  speed, 6, 21, 29
  teeth, 6, 12, 29

ABOUT THE AUTHOR

Charles C. Hofer is a biologist and writer living in New Mexico. He loves cats. However, he's glad he doesn't live with the deadly beasts featured in this book.